· CREATIVE CRAFTS ·

FUN WITH
PAINT

· MOIRA BUTTERFIELD ·

HAMLYN

HANDY HINTS

Some of the paints that you will use to do the painting projects in this book, such as acrylic paints and oil paints, do not wash off easily. You may need to use white spirit to wash them off or to thin them down. Make sure you ask an adult to help you if you use white spirit.

Be very careful when you use sharp scissors or a craft knife for cutting paper and card. Always use a piece of thick cardboard as a cutting board and press downwards when you use a craft knife. Ask an adult to help if you are cutting very thick cardboard.

ACKNOWLEDGEMENTS

Paintings made by Brian Robertson,
Katie Scampton and Anne Sharples
Photographs by David Johnson
Illustrations by Elizabeth Kerr and Joanna Venus

HAMLYN CHILDREN'S BOOKS
Series Editor : Anne Civardi
Series Designer : Anne Sharples
Production Controlller : Linda Spillane

Published in 1993 by
Hamlyn Children's Books
an imprint of Reed International Books Ltd,
Michelin House, 81 Fulham Road, London SW3 6RB

ISBN 0 600 57553 5

Books printed and bound by Proost, Belgium

CONTENTS

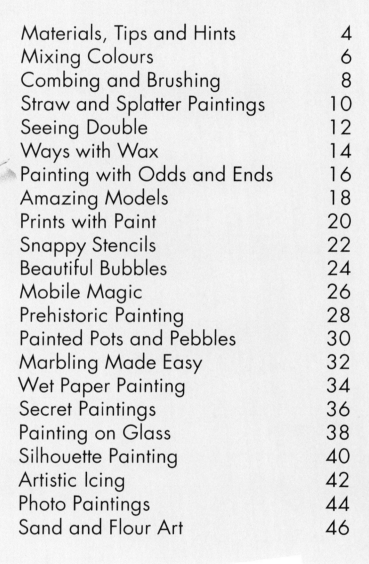

MATERIALS, TIPS AND HINTS

In this book there are lots of different painting projects for you to try. You can probably find most of the things you need for them around the house, but for some you may have to buy things from a toy shop or craft shop. As well as simple step-by-step directions for every project, there are lots of extra handy hints which help you to do them really well.

For most painting you need poster paints or water colours, but a few projects need special kinds of paint, such as acrylic or oil paints. You will also need fat and thin paintbrushes and special brushes for stencilling.

Poster paint is water-based and washes off easily. It is the cheapest kind of paint to buy.

Powdered poster paint needs to be mixed with water.

Ready-mixed poster paint is sold in pots. You can buy big pots and pour out a little at a time.

You can also buy poster paint in small, hard blocks which you mix with water.

Oil paints are the most expensive. They come in small tubes and you do not have to mix them with water.

Brushes, paper and pots

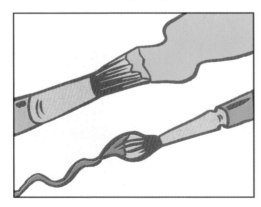

1. Some brushes have flat ends and some have pointed ends. Flat ends are good for painting the backgrounds. Pointed brushes are good for painting thin lines.

2. Some brushes have soft bristles and some have much harder, prickly bristles. It is best to try out different kinds of brushes for different projects.

3. Always wash your brushes in soapy water when you have finished using them. Otherwise they will dry hard, and the bristles will stick together.

Acrylic paints do not wash off easily. They are thick and bright and usually sold in tubes or plastic pots.

HANDY HINTS

Painting can be a very messy business. It is a good idea to wear an old shirt or apron to keep you clean. Cover your work surface with old newspaper and put a couple of plastic rubbish bags on the floor, underneath the table.

It is best to paint in a room where there is a sink close by so that you can keep changing your paint water.

Keep a look out for things that might be useful, such as plastic cartons, tin foil, old toothbrushes, cardboard and an old sponge.

Water colour paints are quite expensive. They come in small tubes or blocks which are then mixed with water. It is best to use them on white paper.

4. You will need some small pots for water. Old yoghurt cartons are ideal. An old baking tray will make a very good palette for you to mix your paints on.

5. If you use paper that is too thin, the paint will make it rumple up when it dries. Thick cartridge paper is best. It is cheapest if you buy a pad.

6. PVA glue is best to use because it washes off clothes easily. It looks white and you can buy it in most shops that sell paints for children.

MIXING COLOURS

On these two pages you can find out how to mix paints together to make all sorts of different colours. All you really need are five main colours - yellow, red, blue, black and white to make all the paint colours on the opposite page. Before you start the projects in this book, experiment to see how many colours you can create. Try not to make them look too muddy.

HANDY HINTS

When you have loaded your brush with paint, do not dip it into another colour. Otherwise you will make your paints muddy.

Change the water you use as soon as it gets dirty so that you have nice clean colours to paint with.

If you put the paint on thickly, the colour will be dark and rich. The more water you mix into the paint, the more delicate the colour will look.

Experiments with colour

1. A light colour looks extra-bright against a dark background. Try putting white paint on top of black paper and see how strong the white paint looks.

2. You can make all sorts of different shades from one colour, depending on how thick or thin the paint is. Try painting a whole picture with just one colour.

3. Pastel shades are colours that are mixed with white. Pale pink, pale blue and pale yellow are all pastel shades. Try making your own pastel colours.

4. When you paint a picture on white paper, leave some of the white showing. It may help to make your painting look much fresher and cleaner.

5. Experiment by painting rows of patterns using two or three colours, like this. Then you can easily see which colours you like using together best.

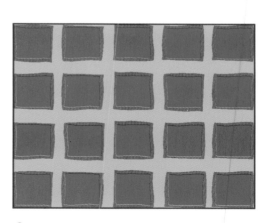

6. Some colours clash with each other, such as red and pink, green or orange. But you can use them together to get a really bright and jazzy effect.

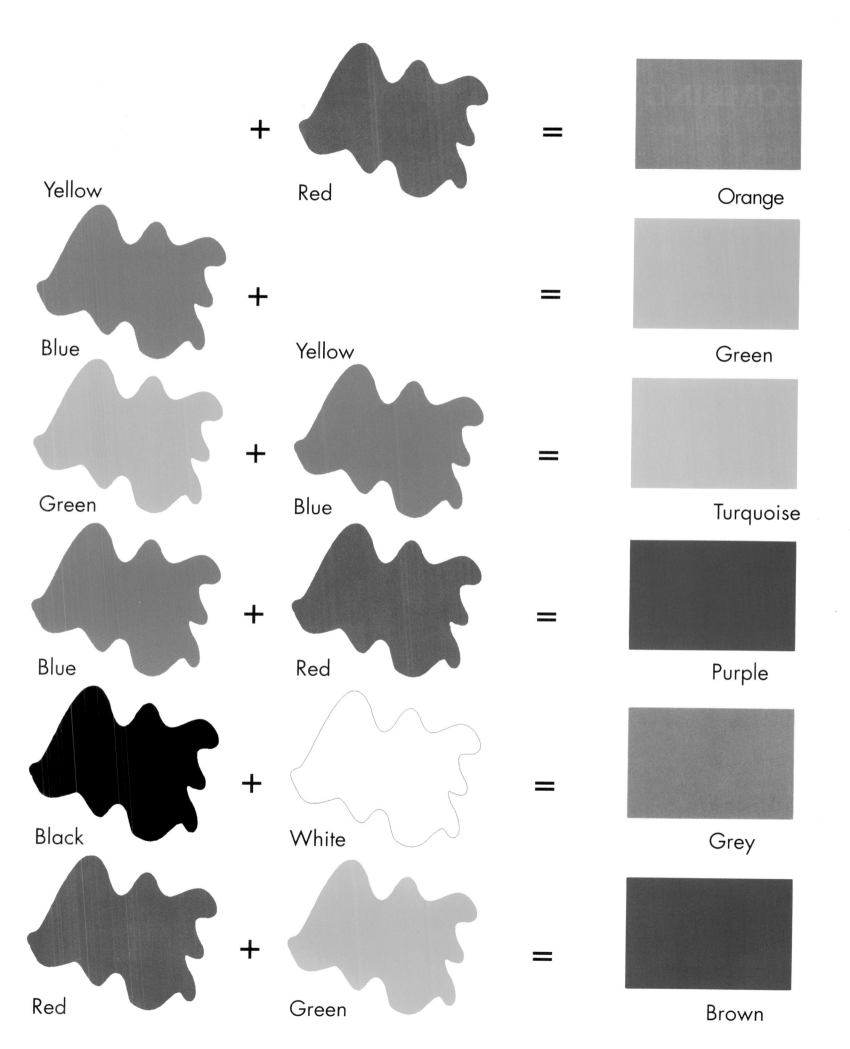

Yellow + Red = Orange

Blue + Yellow = Green

Green + Blue = Turquoise

Blue + Red = Purple

Black + White = Grey

Red + Green = Brown

COMBING AND BRUSHING

You can get all sorts of different patterns and pictures by dragging a comb or a stiff brush across thickly painted paper. Try making your own combs out of thick cardboard, either with blunt teeth or sharp teeth to use as scrapers.

Things you need

Coloured paper
Thin and thick card
Poster paints, including
  gold and silver
Paintbrushes and a palette
A plastic or metal comb
An old hairbrush
Crêpe paper and
  scissors
Thin ribbon

Draw a coiled-up snake. Paint it and then comb patterns in it. Cut out the snake and hang it up.

A golden gift tag

HANDY HINTS

To cover the teeth of a comb or the bristles of a toothbrush with paint, it is easiest to brush the paint on to them with an ordinary paintbrush.

Try putting blobs of paint on to paper and then dragging it into swirls with a comb.

8

Golden gift tag

  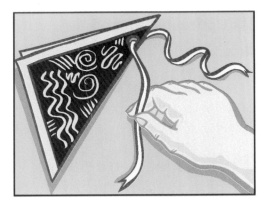

1. Paint a square of paper, about 10 cm by 10 cm, with thick, gold poster paint. Make sure the paint covers the paper completely. Then leave it to dry.

2. Now paint a layer of black paint on top of the gold paint. While this is wet, run the teeth of a comb across it, pressing down to make different patterns.

3. When the paint is dry, cut out the square shape. Fold it in half, diagonally. To make a gift tag, poke a hole in one corner and thread thin ribbon through it.

Perfect party chains

Perfect party chains

1. Cut two long strips of crêpe paper, 3 cm wide. Cover the teeth of a comb or bristles of a hairbrush with paint. Brush or dot them on to the strips.

2. Let the paint dry and then decorate the other side. When they are dry, lay the strips at right-angles and overlap them, like this. Tape down the ends.

3. Pull out the finished chain to use as a party decoration. You can decorate red and green crêpe paper to make all sorts of perfect Christmas decorations.

STRAW AND SPLATTER PAINTINGS

You can have great fun making all sorts of splodgy paintings using straws, toothbrushes or nailbrushes. Use bright coloured paper as well as white to make some interesting patterns. It is best to wear an apron and cover the floor or table with newspaper as it can be a bit messy.

Things you need

Poster paints and a palette
Sheets of white and coloured paper
Drinking straws, an old toothbrush,
  a nailbrush and paintbrushes
Plenty of water and newspaper

HANDY HINTS

Practise putting lots of colours together when you spray or splodge on paint and see the strange effects you can get.

Cut out different card shapes and lay them on the paper before you splatter it with paint. They will leave clear shapes on your picture.

A splodgy straw painting

Blowing with straws

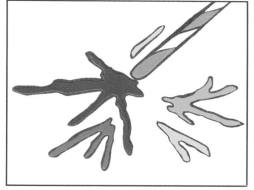

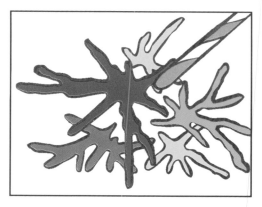

1. Mix up your paints with plenty of water to make them runny. Splatter some paint on to your paper with a paintbrush, or paint on runny lines.

2. Blow the runny paint all over the page using a stiff drinking straw. Dab some extra water on to the paper if the paint is not quite runny enough.

3. Gradually splatter on more colours. If you do this while the paint is wet, the different colours will mix together as you blow them around the paper.

10

Splatter paint through a stencil to make these pictures.

Dab thick paint on some paper with the end of a straw to make apple trees.

Lost in space

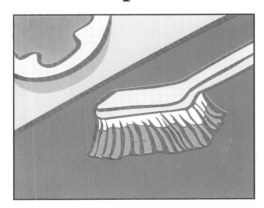

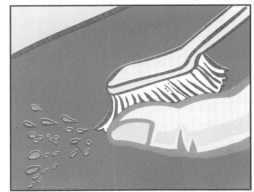

1. To make a starry sky, dab an old toothbrush into some white or orange paint. Hold it over a sheet of dark blue or black paper with the bristles facing down.

2. Gently run your finger along the bristles towards you to spray the paint over the paper. (If you do it the other way, you will get sprayed with paint!).

3. Flick some splodges of paint on to the sky with a paintbrush, to make bigger stars. Paint on a moon, shooting stars and rockets using white, gold or silver paint.

11

SEEING DOUBLE

The mirror prints on these two pages are quick and easy to make and every one is different. They are called mirror prints because the pictures on both sides of the folded paper are exactly the same, like the reflection in a mirror. One of the best ways to do them is by using string dipped in paint. The string makes all sorts of swirling patterns on the paper.

Things you need

Sheets of paper, string and poster paints
Old saucers, a paintbrush and a stirrer

Swirling string pictures

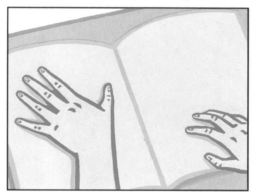

1. Fold a big sheet of white or coloured paper in half. Then smooth it out again, like this, ready to make your picture.

2. Cut two or three short lengths of string. Then put two or three different coloured thick poster paints on to some old saucers.

3. Stir each piece of string into a different colour, as shown. Make sure that they are all completely covered with poster paint.

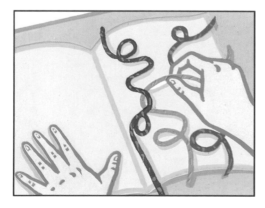

4. Lay the strings down on one side of the paper. Arrange them any way you like, with the ends poking out over one edge.

5. Fold the paper in half again on top of the coils of painted string. Then gently smooth it down with your hand, like this.

6. Hold the paper down with one hand and pull out the strings, one by one, by the ends. Then very carefully open out the paper.

Paint a person on one side and fold the paper over to make these two terrible twins.

To make two fighting monsters, paint a fierce monster facing the middle. Then fold the paper over.

Paint one half of a butterfly, then fold the paper over and press down.

Paint half a castle and then fold over the paper and press down.

Swirling string picture

13

WAYS WITH WAX

Wax crayons are waterproof and do not mix with paint. But if you paint over them with one or two layers of thick paint you can make some unusual pictures and patterns. Use lots of brightly coloured wax crayons and try scratching out this peacock, or make a landscape scene and some paint and wax picture frames.

Things you need

Wax crayons
Water colour or poster paints
A thick paintbrush
Thick paper
Small scissors or a knitting
  needle

This beautiful peacock has been scratched through black poster paint.

Wax and scratch

1. Draw thick bands with different coloured wax crayons on a sheet of paper. Press down hard on the crayons.

2. Paint over the bands of wax with thick, black poster paint until they are completely covered with paint. Let the paint dry.

3. Using a knitting needle or scissors, scratch out a picture through the paint. The coloured wax will show through.

HANDY HINTS

Wax shows up particularly well through thinly painted water colour paint.

It is best to draw your picture first with a pencil. This will not show up when you go over it with a thick layer of wax crayon.

Use water colour paints on wax to make bright patterned picture frames.

Framed wax on wax pictures

Wax on wax

1. To make a scratch picture without paint, cover the paper with a light coloured wax in an oval shape, like this.

2. Cover the pale wax with a darker colour wax. When you scratch out a picture the pale wax will show through.

3. Cut out an oval frame from card for your picture. Decorate the frame with wax and paint over it with thin paint.

PAINTING WITH ODDS AND ENDS

You do not always need a paintbrush to paint a picture. You can get some very strange and interesting effects by dabbing a sponge, cloth or some scrunched-up paper into paint and then pressing them on to paper. Here are some ways to make some special paint patterns.

Things you need

Poster paints, old newspaper and a plate
Tissue paper and an empty crisp packet
Corrugated paper and a kitchen cloth

HANDY HINTS

You can use paper, a sponge, plastic bubble wrap or a textured cloth to make different paint patterns. Look for things around the house to make your own special paint effects.

When you have practised making the patterns, you can use them to paint lots of interesting pictures and Christmas or birthday cards, like the ones in the picture below.

Make cards, gift tags and pictures out of your paintings.

Tissue paper flowers

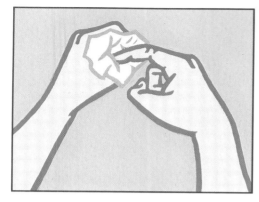

1. Cut a circle out of some tissue paper. Poke the middle of the circle down between your thumb and forefinger to make a paper rosette, as shown.

2. Mix some poster paint on an old plate. Then hold on to the underneath of the rosette, like this, and dab the top gently down into the paint.

3. Press the rosette gently down on to a piece of paper. When you lift it up, there will be a flower shape. Do this again or make different sized circles to make more flowers.

Plastic bag snowstorm

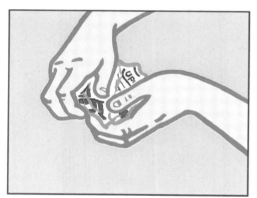

1. Screw up some stiff scrunchy plastic into a ball. An empty crisp packet is best, but a plastic carrier bag may be a little too soft.

2. Mix some white poster paint on an old plate. Then dab the ball of scrunched-up plastic gently down on to the paint.

3. Dab the ball several times on to a piece of thick blue paper to make a splodgy pattern that looks just like falling snow.

More patterns to make

To get patterned lines, use the edge of a piece of corrugated card.

Dab a string cloth on to paint to make a net pattern.

Move a scrunched-up ball of paper from side to side to make swirls.

AMAZING MODELS

These amazing models are all made with things that you can find easily around the house, such as cardboard tubes, egg boxes, milk cartons and empty sweet tubes. Once you have made them, you can paint them brightly with poster paints.

Things you need for the jolly giraffe

5 small cardboard tubes (lavatory rolls are ideal)
A cardboard kitchen roll
An egg box
Corrugated cardboard
String and strong glue
Sticky tape and scissors
Poster paints

Make this strange egg box alien out of an empty egg box with a cardboard roll mouth, cardboard tongue, sweet tube antennae and tin foil hair.

Make a totem pole out of cardboard rolls stuck together and painted. Decorate it with bits of cards.

A jolly giraffe

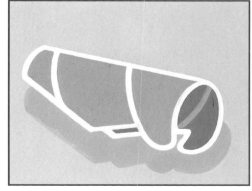

1. Using strong glue, stick a lavatory roll or a small cardboard tube on to each corner of the egg box. These are the giraffe's legs and body. Let the glue dry.

2. To make the neck, cut slits in one end of the cardboard kitchen roll and bend them out. Stick the roll on to the egg box and then tape it down to make it firm.

3. For the giraffe's head, cut a lavatory roll into the shape shown above. Glue it on to the neck and then stick it down with tape to make it firm.

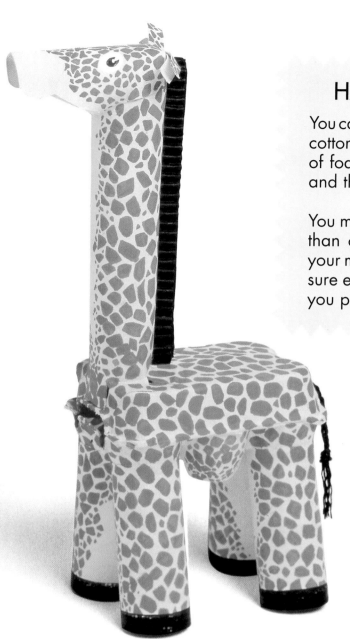

Jolly
giraffe

HANDY HINTS

You can glue things like wool, cotton wool, foil and pieces of foam on to your models, and then paint over them.

You may need to paint more than one layer of paint on your model to cover it. Make sure each layer dries before you paint on the next one.

Make this super spaceship out of ice cream cartons, lavatory rolls and thin cardboard.

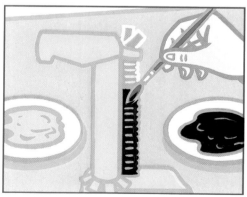

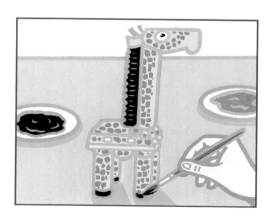

4. For the giraffe's mane, glue a long, thin piece of corrugated cardboard down the back of the neck. Glue on a string tail and fray out the end, as shown.

5. Paint the giraffe's body with yellow poster paint. Let it dry and then paint on a second coat. Paint the mane and tail black. Leave them to dry.

6. Once the yellow paint is dry, paint orange spots all over the jolly giraffe's body. Add two black and white eyes, and four black hooves, like this.

PRINTS WITH PAINT

You can make all sorts of interesting pictures and patterns by printing with leaves, string, vegetables and even biscuits. The secret of making good prints is to use paint that is not too wet, just sticky. Here are some ideas for printing shapes on to paper and fabric.

Things you need

Poster paint
An old tray
A sponge (for a printing pad)
A paintbrush
Different shaped shiny leaves,
   carrots, potatoes, biscuits,
   card and string
A knife

Vegetable print writing
paper and envelopes

Making a print pad

1. Mix some paint with a little water, keeping the paint quite thick and sticky. Put a sponge inside a tray and pour the paint over the sponge.

2. Press vegetable shapes or leaves on to the sponge to cover them with paint. Then press them on to some paper. Rinse out the sponge to change the colour.

Vegetable prints

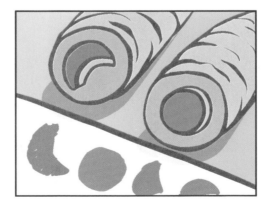

1. Cut a carrot in half. Cut a piece out of one end to leave a raised shape, such as a moon. Make circle prints with one half and moons with the other.

2. Cut a potato in half and pat it dry with a tissue. Cut out a simple shape and use it to print patterns or to decorate writing paper, envelopes and fabric.

HANDY HINTS

To print on fabric you will need special fabric paints. Make sure you put a sheet of newspaper under your work when you start printing.

If you have put on too much paint, dab your printing shape on to newspaper first to make the paint less thick.

Vegetable print moon and stars

Falling leaves

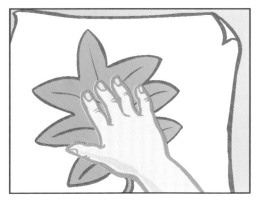

1. Collect different shaped leaves that have a shiny, waxy surface and are nice and strong. Brush paint on to the top of the leaf or use a printing pad.

2. Carefully lay the painted leaf, face-down, on to a piece of plain paper. Press it down gently with your fingers, like this, or with the back of a spoon.

3. Gently peel off the leaf. It will leave a print behind. Make lots of prints with the same leaf in different colours, or try using other kinds of leaves.

SNAPPY STENCILS

Stencilling is a way to make the same picture or pattern over and over again through a piece of card. You can stencil on paper, fabric, wood and even on walls. It is best to practise on an easy shape when you start, such as the clown shape below. Once you have got used to stencilling, you can try some more interesting and complicated ideas.

Things you need

Stiff card or special
  stencil card
Cartridge paper
Small sharp scissors or
  a craft knife
Thick paint
A stencil brush or a
  paintbrush with
  stiff bristles
A piece of natural
  sponge

HANDY HINTS

Try to paint inwards from the outside edge of the stencil hole.

Keep the paint thick. If it is too runny, it will seep underneath the stencil edges and smudge.

You do not always need to dab on an even coat of paint. You can get all sorts of different textures by letting your brush gradually run out of paint as you dab it on.

Cut-out clown stencil

A cut-out clown

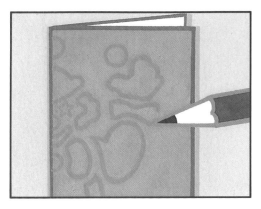

1. Fold a piece of stiff card in half. Draw one half of the clown along the fold line, like this. Cut around the clown shape and then open up the card again.

2. Hold the stencil down firmly with one hand on to some cartridge paper. Then dab the paint on, inside the clown shape, with a special stencil brush.

3. You can use different colours for different parts of the clown. But make sure that you allow each colour to dry before you take the stencil card away.

Make a border by repeating the stencil pattern again and again.

A stencil pattern

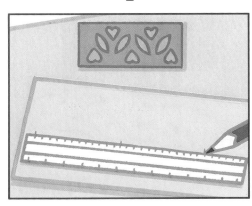

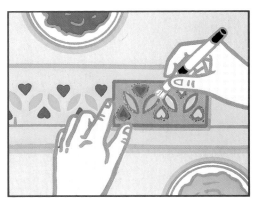

1. Cut out a simple pattern from some card about 12 cm long. Then draw a straight pencil line on the paper you want to stencil. Make 12 cm marks along the line.

2. Put the stencil card on the paper, with the bottom edge of the card running along the line, like this. This will help you to keep the pattern straight.

3. Dab paint through the stencil and wait for it to dry. Then move the card along, between the marks, and stencil again and again until you have finished.

23

BEAUTIFUL BUBBLES

Bubble painting is a lot of fun and the patterns
you get are different every time. You can use it
to make strange pictures or to decorate sheets of
paper which you can make into all sorts of
useful things. You will need to practise a bit
before you get a perfect bubble painting.

Things you need

Washing-up liquid
Three or four cup-sized
  containers
Lots of straws
Acrylic paints or Indian inks
Paintbrushes for mixing
Thick cartridge paper

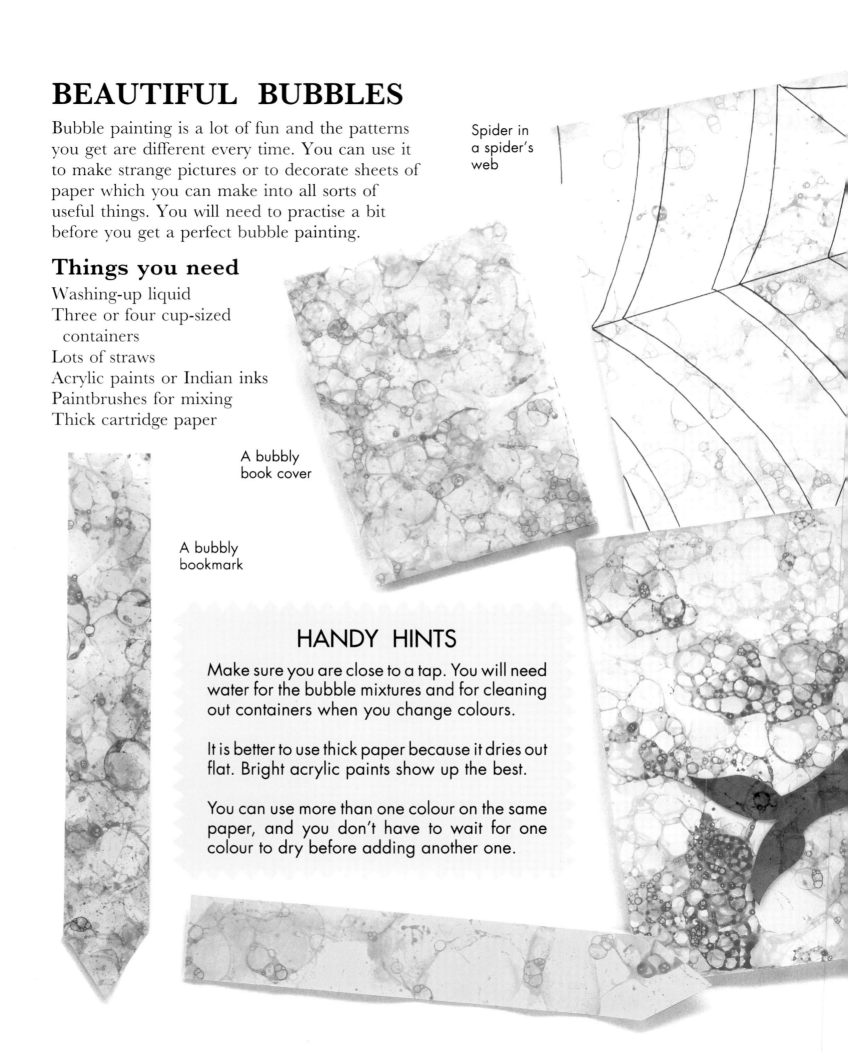

Spider in
a spider's
web

A bubbly
book cover

A bubbly
bookmark

HANDY HINTS

Make sure you are close to a tap. You will need
water for the bubble mixtures and for cleaning
out containers when you change colours.

It is better to use thick paper because it dries out
flat. Bright acrylic paints show up the best.

You can use more than one colour on the same
paper, and you don't have to wait for one
colour to dry before adding another one.

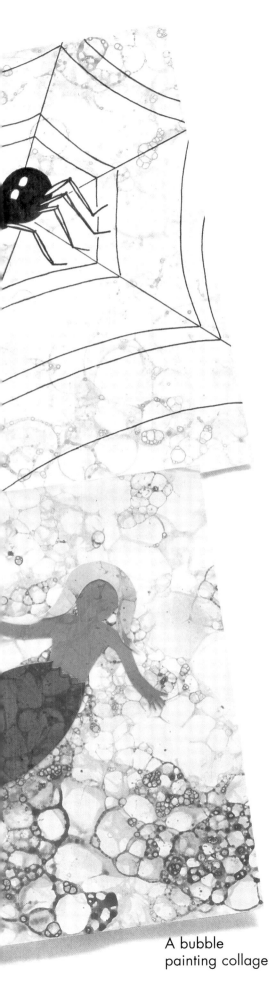

A bubble
painting collage

Blowing bubbles

1. Squeeze about 1½ cm of washing-up liquid into a plastic container. Add a spoonful of wet paint or ink and mix them up.

2. Add a few drops of water. Then blow into the mixture with a straw until it bubbles over the top of the container.

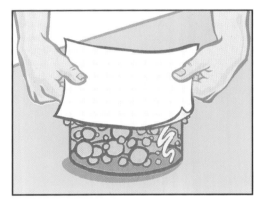

3. Lay the paper on the bubbles for a few seconds. When you lift it off you will see a pattern. Cover the paper with patterns.

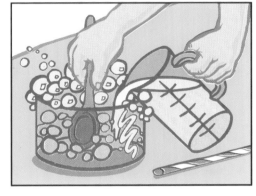

4. If it doesn't work first time, experiment with the bubble mixture. Add more water if it does not bubble properly.

5. If the colour is not strong or bright enough to see, add some more paint or ink to the bubble mixture, as shown.

6. Lay the finished bubble painting out flat on to some newspaper to dry. Make another picture while you are waiting.

MOBILE MAGIC

Here are some ideas on how to make bright and simple mobiles out of card and paint. When you are designing your mobile, choose a theme, such as this fishy mobile, a slithery snake mobile or even a creepy crawly one.

Things you need

Poster paints or acrylic paints
Thin card, scissors and a pencil
Brightly-coloured cotton
  threads and a needle
A big curtain ring

Make a colourful fishy mobile to hang up in the bathroom.

Fishy mobile

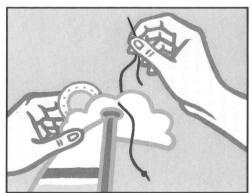

1. Draw a big boat shape, like this, on to some thin card. Then draw six small sea animals, such as an octopus, some fish, a shell, a seahorse and a turtle.

2. Paint all the shapes on one side using lots of different coloured paints. Let the paint dry and then cut out the shapes. Now paint the other sides.

3. Thread the needle and knot one end of the thread. Push the needle through the top of the boat and pull the thread through until the knot stops it.

26

For a creepy crawly mobile, cut out and paint a big sunflower shape. Hang three rows of insects, such as a spider, a caterpillar, a bee, a butterfly, a dragonfly and a worm, from the flower.

HANDY HINTS

Instead of using thread, you can use scraps of brightly-coloured wool. For this you need a needle with a big eye.

You can also hang rows of mobile shapes from a brightly-coloured coat hanger or a wooden coat hanger that you have painted.

Try out some different ways to decorate your mobile shapes, such as splattering or sponging, combing and brushing.

To make a slithery snake mobile, draw a coiled-up snake on some thin card. Cut it out and paint it with bright poster paints. Push some thread through the snake's head. Hang it above a warm radiator to make it move.

4. Thread the needle again and knot one end of the thread. Push the needle through the bottom centre of the boat and pull the thread through, like this.

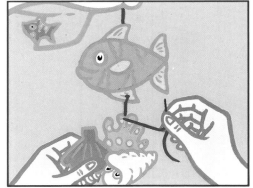

5. Push the needle through the top of a fishy shape. Cut the thread and tie it in a knot so that it hangs down from the boat. Attach another fishy shape.

6. Hang three rows of sea creatures from the boat. Then tie a curtain ring to the thread at the top of the boat and hang it up on a hook.

PREHISTORIC PAINTING

Prehistoric people were the very first artists. They drew on cave walls using colours made from things like charcoal or soil mixed with water. On these two pages there are lots of ideas for making your own natural paints from things you can find outside, or in the kitchen.

Things you need

Thick paper
Brushes or twigs for painting

Colours you can make

Brown	-	tea/coffee and water
Brown	-	soil and water
Black	-	charcoal
Yellow	-	turmeric
Yellow	-	orange peel
Yellow	-	mustard powder and water
Orange	-	chilli powder
Orange	-	carrot
Green	-	grass
Green	-	green pepper juice
Green	-	herbs
Blue	-	cornflower petals
Pink	-	red pepper juice
Red	-	ketchup

Try painting a jungle scene and then outlining it with charcoal.

A natural house and garden

1. For the green grass, pick a handful of grass. Fold it in half and rub it along the bottom of a sheet of white paper. It will make a splodgy green colour.

2. To paint the path, fence and tree trunks, mix some water with a little soil from the garden. Different types of soil will make different shades of brown.

3. Collect some blue coloured flower petals for the sky. Wet them slightly and then rub them along the top of the paper so that their colour comes off.

HANDY HINTS

Mix tea leaves or coffee with water to get a pale brown-beige colour, rather like the colour of old manuscripts.

If you mix coloured powders, such as paprika, with margarine, the mixture spreads out easily and smoothly.

Do not try making paints from any garden berries or fungi of any kind. Some of these are very poisonous. If you use chilli powder, wash your hands well and do not rub your eyes.

A natural house and garden

4. Rub fresh, slightly damp herb leaves, such as parsley or basil, on the paper to get shades of green for the trees. The trees will also smell of the herbs you use.

5. Mix ground kitchen spices, like chilli powder, with soil and water to get yellow and orange colours for the house and roof. Your picture will also smell spicy.

6. To finish your picture, paint on some yellow flowers using a spice called turmeric mixed with water. For pink ones, squeeze the juice out of a red pepper.

PAINTED POTS AND PEBBLES

These colourful flowerpots and pretty pebble paperweights are easy to paint and make good presents. You can decorate lots of other things with paint as well, such as paper plates, wooden spoons, sticks, driftwood and shells.

Things you need

Acrylic paints, paintbrushes and drawing paper
Crayons, a plate and clear gloss varnish
Terracotta flowerpots
Big flat pebbles

Paint a wooden spoon with one colour and then decorate it brightly.

A pretty pot

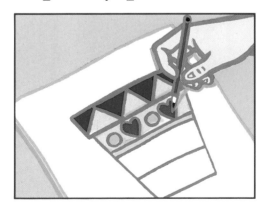

1. Before you start, decide what you want to paint on your pot. Draw a design on some paper and colour it in with crayons. Then put the flowerpot on to an old china plate.

2. If you want a background colour, paint it on to the pot first and let it dry. Then paint your design on top. Use thin brushes for delicate lines and fat ones for bigger patterns.

3. Once the pot is dry, cover it with a clear gloss varnish, using a thick brush. If you want an extra-shiny pot, brush on another coat of varnish. Try painting a face or animal on another pot.

30

Use lots of bright colours when you paint your pots.

HANDY HINTS

Don't worry if you make a mistake while you are decorating your pots and pebbles. Wait until the paint is dry and then paint over the top.

Put your pot or pebble on to a plate to paint it. You can turn the plate around as you paint so that you do not have to touch the wet pot.

Make some strange creatures out of painted pebbles.

For party decorations, paint and varnish paper cups and paper plates.

Pebble paperweights

1. Before you start you will have to find some flat, smooth pebbles or pebbles with odd or interesting shapes. The best place to find them is on a stony beach or close to a river bank.

2. Decide what you want your paperweights to look like. You can paint on faces, patterns and scenes, or make them look like a particular animal, such as a bird, lion, fish, or a spooky insect.

3. Paint the pebble all over with a background colour, using acrylic paint. Let it dry. Then paint on a face or body, like this. When the paint is dry, brush two coats of varnish on to the pebble.

MARBLING MADE EASY

Marbled paper has beautiful patterns and every sheet looks different. It looks difficult to do, but it is really very easy. You can use it as writing paper, for wrapping presents, for covering books and even to make a fabulous fan. Marbling can be a bit messy and you will need to wear an apron and some rubber gloves.

Things you need

Oil-based paints (if you use
    thick oil paints, you need to
    thin them with white spirit)
Rubber gloves and an apron
Thick cartridge paper and
    some newspaper
Two or three paintbrushes
A shallow baking tray, about
    2.5 cm deep
Some vinegar

Marvellous marbled writing set

Strips of marbled paper make good napkin rings.

Make your own special marbled gift tags.

Marbling paper

1. Check that the piece of paper you are going to marble fits into the baking tray. Almost fill the tray with water. Mix in a good splash of vinegar.

2. Use a paintbrush to dribble and splatter different coloured paint on to the water. If it is thin enough, the paint will float on top of the water.

3. Use up to four colours. Try swirling them around with a cocktail stick, blowing the paint around with a straw or adding blobs with a brush.

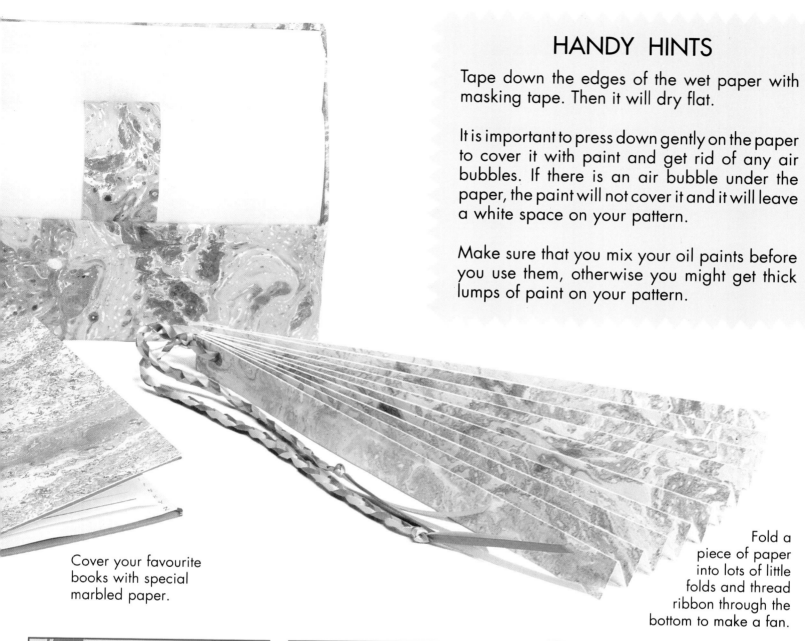

HANDY HINTS

Tape down the edges of the wet paper with masking tape. Then it will dry flat.

It is important to press down gently on the paper to cover it with paint and get rid of any air bubbles. If there is an air bubble under the paper, the paint will not cover it and it will leave a white space on your pattern.

Make sure that you mix your oil paints before you use them, otherwise you might get thick lumps of paint on your pattern.

Cover your favourite books with special marbled paper.

Fold a piece of paper into lots of little folds and thread ribbon through the bottom to make a fan.

4. Gently lay the paper, face down, on to the top of the water. Tap on it very softly with your finger, like this, to get rid of any air bubbles underneath.

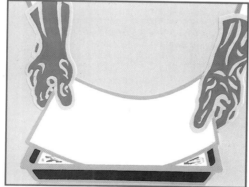

5. After a few moments, lift up the paper with both hands, holding opposite ends. Let the water drain off the paper into the tray below.

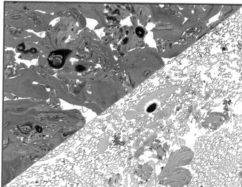

6. Lay the paper on newspaper and let it dry. Before you throw the water away, try some more marbling. The pattern will come out lighter each time.

WET PAPER PAINTING

You can get all sorts of interesting and exciting effects by painting on wet cartridge paper. It is particularly useful for making sky and landscape pictures. Try using poster paints or, for a more watery-looking effect, you can use water colours.

HANDY HINTS

Try brushing lots of different coloured paints on to wet paper. Hold the paper over a sink so that all the colours run together and the extra paint drips off. Turn the paper round to make the colours run in different directions.

Things you need

Paintbrushes and poster paint
Cartridge paper
Water in a container

If you use water colour paints, use water colour paper because it does not crinkle up so much when it dries.

A farmhouse painted on top of a wash background.

A watery landscape

1. Wet a sheet of white cartridge paper by painting all over it with water, as shown. It is best to use a big, fat paintbrush.

2. Still using the big brush, paint on different colours for the land and sky. The colours will mix together as you paint.

3. When your wash painting is dry, use it as a background for painting on a farmhouse, trees, flowers and clouds.

Pale yellow, pink and blue colours are best for painting a sunset sky on wet paper.

Use water colours on wet paper to make a still life picture, like these plums on a plate.

Using water colours

1. Sketch out the basic shapes of the picture you want to paint, using a very light pencil on dry water colour paper.

2. Wet a piece of paper. Then use the water colours to get different effects of light and shade, and dark shadows.

3. If you put one colour next to another, they will run together. Practise first to see what kinds of pictures you can create.

SECRET PAINTINGS

The secret paintings on these two pages change when you want them to. The clever candle pictures are ideal for secret treasure maps, secret letters and spy messages.

Things you need

White paper
Water colour or poster paints
A white candle
A pencil and paintbrush

HANDY HINTS

If you send a secret picture to a friend, don't forget to send them the instructions on how to make the picture appear.

It is best to plan out your hidden painting before you start. You can sketch it first and then paint over the lines.

This valentine heart is done with a red candle on red paper covered with white paint.

Grinning ghostly painting

A secret candle picture

1. Draw a picture or a secret message on some white paper using the tip of a white candle.

2. When you want the picture to appear, paint over it with poster paint or water colours.

3. The paint will not cover the waterproof wax and the white lines will show through.

A hidden
storm

Secret map
of hidden
treasure

Hidden storm painting

1. Draw and then paint a picture, such as this boat in a storm, on a rectangular piece of paper. Let the paint dry.

2. Fold over about one-third of the paper. Complete the picture on the blank part, so that it joins up with the first picture.

3. Make some changes to the things you show on the folded part. When you open the flap, the picture will change.

PAINTING ON GLASS

If you paint a picture on a window, the light shines through it to make the colours glow like stained glass. Poster paints are best to use because they can be wiped off with water, but you can also use acrylic paints. You can paint pictures and patterns on jars, glasses and bottles.

Things you need

Poster or acrylic paints
A palette
Different-sized paintbrushes
A ruler

A flowery glass

Birds in a tree bottle and glass

Blooming window box

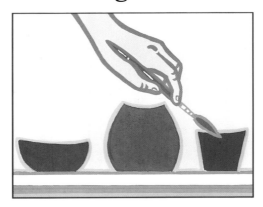

1. Choose a window to paint on. Mix up the colours you want to use and paint some pots along the bottom of the window. Let them dry and then decorate them.

2. Paint bright flowers above the pots, either with a brush or by dabbing on wet paint with a scrunched-up tissue, like this. Paint a spiky cactus, too.

3. Paint on stalks and different sized and shaped leaves, using several shades of green. Paint in some flower middles and some black spikes on the cactus.

Noah's weather
window

Blooming
window box

HANDY HINTS

You can make lines and squiggles on the window by scratching gently on to the wet paint with the end of a paintbrush.

Use thick paint to stop drips. If the paint does drip you can wipe it off and start again.

You can buy paints made especially for painting on glass. Remember to read the instructions well and to be very careful when you use them.

Super sailing
ship

Sweet
scent
bottles

Noah's weather window

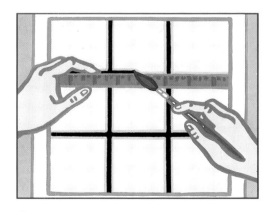

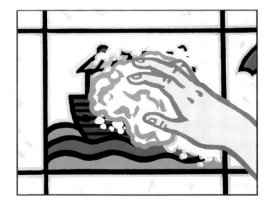

1. Paint nine squares in black paint to look like the black lead in a stained glass window. Run your brush along a ruler edge to get nice straight lines.

2. Paint a different picture inside each square. Noah's window has an ark, weather symbols, such as sun, rain and snow, as well as an umbrella and a snowman.

3. If you want to change the pictures in the future, do the black lines with acrylic paint. They will stay when you wipe off the poster paint pictures.

SILHOUETTE PAINTING

On a dark afternoon, paint a silhouette picture of a friend. Silhouette paintings are really dark shadows or outlines painted on a much lighter background. To make them nice and bright, use lots of different colours. You can also draw around figures cut out from old magazines and then paint in the figure shapes.

Things you need

Paper
Acrylic or thick poster paint
Paintbrushes and a palette
A pair of scissors
Cut-out figures from old
   magazines or catalogues

Cut out and frame silhouettes of your friends.

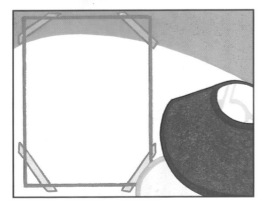

Face silhouette

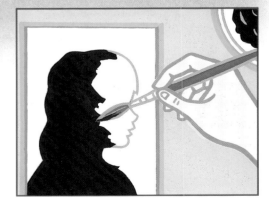

1. Close the curtains or wait until it is dark outside. Switch on a light. Then tape some paper on to the wall, or prop it up so that it is at head height.

2. Ask a friend to stand sideways in front of the paper so that the side of their face casts a sharp shadow outline on the paper. He should not be too close.

3. Paint around the outline, or draw around it and paint the line afterwards. Take the paper down and paint in the head shape. Label the silhouette.

Figure
silhouettes

HANDY HINTS

If you are doing a face silhouette, try moving your friend closer or further away from the paper. When you move him, his silhouette will change shape and become bigger or smaller.

You can also paint a person's silhouette just by looking at them from the side, without using a shadow to help you.

You can cut out figures from a magazine, arrange them on some plain paper and paint around the edges with thick paint.

Ask a friend to stand left and then right for this double silhouette.

Figure silhouettes

1. Cut out some figures from an old magazine or catalogue. Arrange them any way you like on top of a sheet of white paper. Leave space around each figure.

2. Hold one of the figures down while you carefully draw around it with a sharp pencil so that you have the outline of a figure. Do the same with the other cut-outs.

3. When you have covered the paper with figures, paint inside the outlines with lots of different colours. Try using other shapes cut out from old magazines.

ARTISTIC ICING

These two pages give you lots of ideas for painting on food, especially cakes and buns, using white icing and food colouring. You can easily make your own icing or buy ready-made icing in tubes at the supermarket.

Things you need

White icing (see recipe)
A rolling pin and pastry shape cutters
Food colourings (the paste type is best)
Thin paintbrushes and a wooden board
A plate or tray
Plain sponge cup cakes

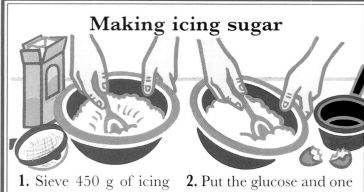

Making icing sugar

1. Sieve 450 g of icing sugar into a bowl. Make a well in the middle. Warm 50 g of glucose until it is slightly runny.

2. Put the glucose and one egg white into the well. Gradually beat it all together until stiff. Knead it until it is smooth.

Iced and painted cup cakes

Painted cup cakes

1. Roll out some icing on to a board. Cut out round shapes to fit the tops of some cup cakes. Brush the cakes with jam or honey and stick the icing on.

2. Using food colourings, paint a different picture on each iced cake top. You can mix the food colourings together, or with water to make them paler.

3. Before you serve the cakes, put them on a plate or tray in the fridge for about 24 hours, or until the paint is completely dry on the icing.

Icing
animals

HANDY HINTS

Wrap your icing in cling film and put it in the fridge until you are ready to use it. The more you knead it, the softer it becomes.

To roll out icing, dust a wooden board and rolling pin with icing sugar. With clean hands, knead the icing a little to soften it and then roll it to the thickness you want.

Christmas decorations

An icing cat

1. Roll some icing into two balls, one larger than the other. Make sure the icing is not too soft. Squash the bigger ball down on to a plate. This is the cat's body.

2. Press the smaller ball on to the cat's body, to make its head. Squeeze around the joins with your finger and a little water to stick the two firmly together.

3. Add some icing ears and a tail, as shown, and then paint the cat in tabby colours. Paint on a face and some whiskers. Put the cat in the fridge until it dries.

PHOTO PAINTINGS

Surprise your family and friends with these unusual photo paintings. They are very easy to do and make good presents. All you need are photographs, paper or card and some poster paints. You can also make a special advent calendar for Christmas using lots of pictures cut out of magazines.

Things you need

Thick paper or card
Poster paints or water colours
Strong glue and scissors
Photographs of your family, friends or pets
Pictures cut out of magazines

Make a special good luck card.

A full house

A full house

1. Paint a picture of a house, with six small windows and a door. When the paint is dry, cut the windows and door on three sides to make flaps, like this.

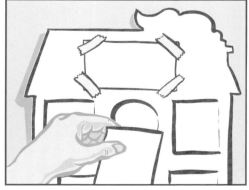

2. Stick photographs of your family or friends underneath the flaps from behind. When you open the flaps you will be able to see all their faces.

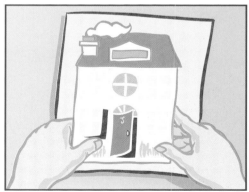

3. When it is dry, spread glue on to the back of the picture. Then stick the full house down on to a big sheet of brightly coloured stiff paper or card, like this.

Fashion figures

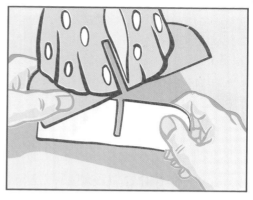

1. Cut the head off a photograph or off a picture of a person in a magazine, such as your favourite pop star. Stick the head on to a sheet of card, like this.

2. Paint some clothes or a silly costume underneath the head. Then cut out the whole figure, as well as a rectangular shape at the bottom, as shown.

3. Cut a slit in the middle of the rectangular piece of card. Slide another piece into it to make a stand. Glue them together to make the stand firm.

Fashion figures

Fold up a strip of paper. Stick a different face on to each fold and decorate the backgrounds.

HANDY HINTS

If you make an advent calendar, it will need 24 windows and a door. Cut out some Christmas pictures from magazines to put behind them. Open one window each day until you reach the door, December 25th.

SAND AND FLOUR ART

Poster paint mixed with sand or flour makes thick, bumpy paint. It is especially good for painting model scenes, such as landscapes or seascapes. You can also press leaves, twigs or shells on to the paint before it dries to get an even more realistic scene.

Things you need

Poster paint and paintbrushes
Clean, dry sand
Flour
Thick smooth paper or card
A plastic picnic knife

A smiling sandy hippo

A sandy scene

A sandy scene

1. Mix some poster paints with sand. Do not make the mixture too thick, or it will stick to your brush and will not spread very easily over the paper.

2. Build up a picture from the top of the page, starting with the sky. Then paint some mountains, the grass and the trees. Finish off with the sand and sea.

3. Use a picnic knife to lay the mixture on thickly. Try making waves and cuts in it as well. It is best to use the tip of a brush to draw lines and squiggles.

4. Press all kinds of things, such as twigs, leaves or tin foil, on to the picture. For extra texture, sprinkle more sand on top of the wet mixture, as shown.

5. If you add flour and water to the sand mixture it spreads much more thinly over a wide area. A mixture of flour and water makes good clouds and snow.

6. Leave your picture to dry overnight. When it is dry, you could rub some areas smooth with your finger. Then shake off any extra sand.

PRINTED IN BELGIUM BY

INTERNATIONAL BOOK PRODUCTION